# CLOSE to HOME

*The landscapes, wildlife and hidden beauty
of central Illinois*

Published by The State Journal-Register
One Copley Plaza, Springfield, Illinois 62705-0219

Printed in the United States of America
by Phillips Brothers Printers
Springfield, Illinois

First printing October 2000
Second printing November 2000

Library of Congress Catalog Number: 00-105746

ISBN: 0-9675600-1-2

Copies of this book can be ordered through The State Journal Register's Web site: www.sj-r.com, or by contacting Nancy Evans in the promotion department at (217) 788-1356.

On the cover: A field of sunflowers blooms at the Jim Edgar Panther Creek State Fish and Wildlife Area.

 14

# CLOSE to HOME

*The landscapes, wildlife and hidden beauty of central Illinois*

PHOTOGRAPHY *by* CHRIS YOUNG

PUBLISHED *by* THE STATE JOURNAL-REGISTER

# IN MEMORY

*This book is dedicated to my grandfather,*

GEORGE STANLEY,

*and my father-in-law,*

PHIL RILEY.

*Both men gave me my appreciation for the great outdoors.*

# CONTENTS

**At sunset, the familiar form of a great blue heron stands out against the water at Sangchris Lake State Park.**

# FOREWORD

The idea to assemble a collection of Chris Young's photographs began with a call from friend and local architect Earl W. "Wally" Henderson Jr.: "You should do a book," Wally called to say, "of State Journal-Register photographs." A longtime admirer of quality photojournalism, Wally thought a book of pictures would be a grand idea.

Not that his suggestion was wrong, but when one considers the thousands of wonderful images that have been published over the newspaper's 169-year history, it's hard to get an idea of just where to begin. There are so many fine photographs that a book of 1,000 pages wouldn't begin to accommodate the collection.

There is, however, one universally appreciated specialty among the newspaper's legendary photojournalism — Chris Young's photographs of the natural world. Suddenly, the theme for Wally Henderson's picture book had a very clear focus.

Barely a day passes that in some way Chris's magnificent images of birds, animals or the central Illinois landscape aren't mentioned by an appreciative newspaper reader. On many days, nestled amid disturbing news reports from around the world, we find one of Chris's pictures, and in an instant are brought momentary peace. Perhaps it's a white-tailed deer peering curiously through a winter wonderland at Lake Springfield, or a majestic bald eagle soaring above the Illinois River, or a sea of sunflowers bursting with late-summer brilliance. Whatever the image, we are often moved by its beauty, or by the complexity and majesty of nature. We are comforted by the message contained in a simple photograph. For this, many of us pay Chris's work the highest possible tribute — we post it on the refrigerator door.

As a former newspaper photographer, I have great respect and admiration for the art — and the power — of photojournalism. As a means of communication, there is no more enduring vehicle, for unlike the fleeting nature of video or of conversation, a picture freezes a moment in time and is available for us to absorb time and time again. The successful photograph, felt from the photographer's heart and composed through eyes blessed with sensitivity, has the power to move us in many directions. Indeed, pictures can be worth a thousand words, sometimes many thousands more.

Chris Young's photographs speak volumes about the natural world in central Illinois. They serve as an eloquent reminder of the fragile relationship that exists between man and the world around him, and they offer subtle encouragement for the protection of that relationship.

Though much of what Chris has captured on film is oftentimes available for viewing right in our own back yards, finding the time to look can be difficult. He's brought it all to us in this delightful collection of images.

Thanks, Chris. The pleasure is ours.

—*Barry Locher*
*Editor*
*The State Journal-Register*

It just wouldn't be Washington Park without squirrels. Fox and gray squirrels are especially active in the fall, when they busy themselves collecting acorns.

# AN INVITATION

Almost 200 years ago, Lewis and Clark set out on a journey to explore the western half of our country. Since then, it would seem, we've investigated every nook and cranny from coast to coast. Railroads, and later interstate highways, crisscrossed the nation and we now can travel in comfort and ease to formerly remote locations.

Therefore, most people would answer "no" to the question, "Are there any places left unexplored in the United States?"

Yet, I recently stood underneath a tree in Springfield's Washington Park, looking up at a family of barred owls. People all around me were bicycling, walking dogs, fishing or relaxing in the sunshine, and had no knowledge of the owls' presence. It occurred to me that there are many discoveries still to be made right here.

So often we feel the need to travel elsewhere to fulfill our urge to explore. Mountains and seashores may offer more exotic natural treasures, but I've learned that, with a little effort, a wealth of beauty can be found nearby. Owls can live right in

**A barred owl chick (left) and its parent peer out from a secluded perch in Washington Park.**

the middle of town. An incredible variety of delicate wildflowers blooms every spring. These weren't revelations to science, of course, but they were to me.

Almost every week, I take time between my assignments for The State Journal-Register to drive around country roads or take a walk at Lake Springfield. Afterward

I'll page through my field guides, trying to determine what I have photographed. When that fails, I rely on the experts at the Illinois Department of Natural Resources, the Illinois State Museum or local naturalists to answer my questions.

Nearly all of the photographs in this book have been taken in The State Journal-Register's circulation area, which covers 13 counties in central Illinois. The white squirrels of Olney and the prairie chickens in Jasper County are among the few that fall outside this boundary. The white squirrels are included because they represent a community's pride in a unique natural occurrence. The prairie chickens are a symbol of the vast prairie that once covered the midsection of our state, and our current efforts to restore some of that natural heritage.

This book is an invitation to explore this area's hidden beauty. I hope you are inspired to begin your own search for little discoveries — close to home.

—*Chris Young*

Birdwatchers from as far away as Chicago came to Community Park in Rochester in January 2000 to view a Bohemian waxwing. The bird was flocking with 70-150 cedar waxwings. Bohemian waxwings are slightly larger with a gray underside and are reddish-brown under the tail. The Bohemian waxwing was hundreds of miles away from its usual range, and was only the third one recorded in Sangamon County in the past 30 years.

Mist rolls off Lake Springfield on a January evening as the temperature drops below zero.

**A white-tailed deer emerges from a snowy scene at the Wildlife Sanctuary near Lake Springfield.**

Ducks paddle through a painterly scene at Chautauqua National Wildlife Refuge near Havana.
Partially submerged vegetation serves as nature's brush strokes.

Above: A great blue heron blends in with its surroundings at Lake Springfield. The largest and most widespread of the herons found here, it hunts by walking stealthily through shallow water, then grabs — with lightning speed — small fish, frogs, birds and insects (below).

Along the Sangamon River near Decatur, a broken tree limb makes an ideal perch for this juvenile barred owl.

A tiny field sparrow seeks shelter at the edge of a field near Sangchris Lake State Park.

The brilliant white plumage of great egrets stands in stark contrast to the deep shadows of a wooded shoreline in Chautauqua National Wildlife Refuge near Havana.

Ducks explode into flight at the Sanganois Conservation Area near Chandlerville. The Sanganois serves a dual role, part set aside as a refuge and another section for public hunting.

**A juvenile red-tailed hawk takes wing near Lake Springfield.**

A white-tailed deer looks over its shoulder as it heads across the golf course at the Eagle Creek Resort and Conference Center near Lake Shelbyville.

# A WALK IN THE WOODS

**A raccoon ventures out at twilight in the Lick Creek Wildlife Preserve.**

It always pays to listen to the words of children; they often get right to the heart of the matter.

On assignment to photograph a volunteer at Adams Wildlife Sanctuary in Springfield years ago, I was tagging along with a group of school kids on a nature walk. The volunteer guide was pointing out the various plants, birds, insects and other signs of life. She also took care to show the children the many creatures living in decaying tree branches and other debris on the forest floor.

A girl standing near the rear of the group made an astute observation. "There sure is a lot of dead stuff here," she said.

That's true, I thought. In natural areas, fallen trees aren't cleared away like they are in town. The leaves aren't vacuumed up and the grass isn't mowed. As our population has shifted from rural areas to the cities, we've left behind some of our understanding of nature as well as our connection to it.

Those dead trees are essential to life. Woodpeckers bore holes looking for insects to eat. Cavity-nesting birds like screech owls and chickadees take over when the woodpeckers move on. Brown creepers seek shelter in the spaces where bark has separated from tree trunks. Tiny wood-boring insects slowly reduce the wood to soil. Then, in the spring, wildflowers rise out of the decay of the forest floor to complete the cycle of life.

A walk in the woods can help repair that connection to nature and remind us of the ways life always seems to triumph.

Even a brief stroll can bring rewards.

One trail I set out to explore along Lake Springfield was only about 50 yards long, but that didn't matter to me. A fallen tree made a comfortable seat, and within 10 minutes, four white-tailed deer materialized out of the woods to take a drink, explore and play along the shoreline. Fifteen minutes and two rolls of film later, the deer were gone and I was left to ponder my good fortune.

**White-tailed deer warily make their way along the shore of Lake Springfield.**

Tracks found in the snow may be the only evidence of the previous night's activities. Here a raccoon has left its footprints on a downed tree in the Lick Creek Wildlife Preserve.

A red-tailed hawk finds a secluded place for a snack along the Sangamon River near Decatur.

Hermit thrushes are easily identified by their rusty red tails, which they can flick to a higher position, then gradually lower to normal. This one was seen in the Lick Creek Wildlife Preserve at Lake Springfield.

Still covered mostly with down, this pair of great horned owl chicks is just starting to grow flight feathers. Baby owls, like other birds, often venture out of the nest before they are able to fly.

The common yellowthroat is easily identified by its black mask. Its song is easily confused with that of a wren.

**Above:** Eastern bluebirds, like this one at the edge of Lake Springfield's Wildlife Sanctuary, build their nests in old woodpecker holes and other cavities. They have been helped in recent years by the establishment of nest boxes that replace nesting cavities lost when dead trees and fence posts are removed.

**Right:** A magnolia warbler cuts loose with a song along a trail in Washington Park. Warblers are woodland species that stop In central Illinois during spring and fall migrations.

# SPRING IN CARPENTER PARK

**Spring beauties are identified by the long, narrow leaves found halfway up the stem. They are among the earliest flowers to bloom.**

Early in April, wildflowers seize upon a brief window of opportunity.

The trees haven't yet gained their leaves. Sunlight can still penetrate the forest canopy, and those delicate little flowers and plants on the forest floor take center stage.

Familiar wildflowers like Dutchman's breeches, May apples, prairie trillium and spring beauties provide some of the first color of the year in Springfield's Carpenter Park.

This park originally was a tract of land owned by William Carpenter in 1838. Carpenter had a cabin on the Sangamon River where he built a sawmill and gristmill. In 1921, his daughter donated the land to the city of Springfield, and it was dedicated as a nature preserve in the 1970s.

All plants and animals in the park are protected by law. To keep the park as natural as possible, only foot traffic is allowed. No bicycles, motorized vehicles, horses or dogs are permitted.

By the time late May and the beginning of summer are upon us, Carpenter Park's forest canopy has closed. Those delicate spring wildflowers have packed up their show: They've sprouted, bloomed, been pollinated and gone to seed.

They're already preparing for next year's performance.

Dutchman's breeches, aptly named for blooms that look like upside-down pantaloons, are a familiar sign of spring in the wood-lands of Carpenter Park.

Tree limbs may still be bare in April, but the forest floor is lush and green in Carpenter Park.

Trails chewed by hungry insects create a distinctive pattern much like a computer's circuit board.

May apples blanket the forest floor in Carpenter Park. The drooping leaves conceal a single bloom that gives way to a small "apple" later. Beware: While the fruit is edible and can be made into jelly, the rest of the plant — including leaves, roots and seeds — is poisonous.

A white trout lily emerges from the recently burned forest floor at Carpenter Park.

**Above: Prairie trillium blooms at the edge of a trail in Carpenter Park.**

**Right: The light purple flowers of blue phlox add color to the green forest floor. Early wildflowers, called "spring ephemerals," last only a few weeks until trees fill with leaves and the canopy of the forest shuts off sunlight.**

A comma butterfly lights on decaying oak leaves.

# ALONG THE WAY:
## *Roadside wildlife*

Growing up in rural Iowa, I used to roll my eyes at the old-timers who drove slowly up and down country roads, checking out the progress of their neighbor's crops.

Now that old-timer is me. These days, I'm cruising just as slowly for pictures.

It seems that a car serves as a surprisingly good blind when it comes to watching wildlife.

Apparently, birds and animals are used to passing cars. It's only when the occupant gets out that the routine changes, and critters hightail it to safety.

When I'm driving along lightly traveled country roads, it's possible to pull over and observe for a moment without having my subjects pay too much attention. As soon as I have my pictures, however, I move on before I wear out my welcome.

I never expected that roadsides would provide such a variety of nature photographs. But consider the fact that most of central Illinois is tillable,

and therefore serves as cropland. It stands to reason that the grass along the roads would provide a significant portion of habitat for wildlife.

With that said, here's a conservation tip that requires absolutely no action at all on your part or mine: *Leave ditches and roadsides unmowed in summer until at least August.* By putting off roadside mowing, grassland species of game and non-game wildlife can successfully nest and raise young.

Some areas need to be mowed, of course. An apron strip can be mowed along the shoulder so farmers can see where they are going when driving big machinery.

And areas that need to be mowed for safety and visibility, such as intersections, can be mowed in spring, then kept short to discourage nesting.

But instead of mowing those ditches this summer, have another cool lemonade and pat yourself on the back for a job well done.

And make sure to wave at me from the porch when I cruise by. I'll be the one moving especially slowly.

**Above: Prairie flowers bloom at Jim Edgar Panther Creek State Fish and Wildlife Area, formerly known as Site M.**

**Facing page: Northern bobwhites dash for the cover of roadside grasses near the town of Bluff Springs in Cass County. Many species of grassland birds rely on unmowed ditches and roadsides for nesting habitat.**

Facing page: A dickcissel belts out a song in a field near Sangchris Lake State Park. Dickcissels are found in huge flocks during migration, when they travel as far as South America. In summer, they can be found in grain fields, prairies and weedy lots.

Left: An eastern meadowlark announces its presence at Sangchris Lake State Park.

**The hunter and the hunted: A red-tailed hawk stops for a roadside meal near Lake Springfield. Facing page: A cottontail rabbit is alert to danger.**

These familiar faces are fixtures along roadways. Indigo buntings (facing page) are often found in hedgerows and brushy areas. The males are easy to spot due to their iridescent blue color. Above: A red-winged blackbird guards its territory from the only perch available in a grassy field.

A great spangled fritillary searches for nectar on the flower of a common milkweed.

Eastern kingbirds are often seen perched at roadsides where they hunt for insects all summer.

# VANISHING GRASSLANDS:
## Reminders of our Prairie Heritage

Short-eared owls were once among the most plentiful owl species in Illinois. In the days before settlement, prairie grasses covered much of the state, and the short-eared owl was well-adapted to the landscape.

They hovered and fluttered over the prairies in search of voles to eat. They built their nests on the ground in this land of few trees, the only owl in Illinois to do so.

Today, less than 1 percent of the original prairie remains. To see a short-eared owl in the wild is a fairly unusual event.

Two groups of short-eared owls spent the winter in central Illinois recently. One group was seen near Chatham and another near Farmersville. Their presence gave wildlife-watchers hope that things may be going in the right direction, and that short-eared owls and other prairie species may one day return to Illinois in greater numbers.

Scientists, however, will tell you that one year does not qualify as a statistical trend. My field guide also advises cautious

**Top: Larger animals that once roamed Illinois, like these bison, can only be seen in living history museums. Above: Not yet rejuvenated by spring, prairie grasses sway in the breeze at Carpenter Park.**

optimism: "Short-eared owls can vary in abundance from year to year," it says.

Those who saw the group wintering near Chatham, however, noted that the owls were living in a wide, grassy strip planted to filter agricultural chemicals before they reach a creek feeding into Lake Springfield. The grass also helps prevent erosion. Sixty feet wide on each side of the creek, the filter strips meant to protect the water supply

may be protecting wildlife as well.

Like short-eared owls, northern harriers are also a state-endangered species. That means very few pairs choose Illinois as a place to nest and raise a family. Migrants are seen in spring and fall, but there are few full-time residents.

To see a northern harrier hunt a field is a privilege. Flying back and forth just a few feet above the ground, harriers often stop to hover over a spot where a potential meal may be hiding. Aviation buffs note that the harrier jet, which can take off and land vertically, borrows its name from this grassland hawk.

I watched a northern harrier hunt a field on a country road somewhere between Bath and Patterson Bay. I slowly backed my car down a dirt lane and took a few pictures, then backed up a little more as it moved on.

To avoid a ditch, I quickly glanced behind me. But when I turned back to the field, the harrier was gone. In that instant, the hunt must have been successful. The hawk had vanished from view, hiding somewhere in the grass with its dinner.

This state-endangered short-eared owl was among a group of about 15 that spent the winter just east of Farmersville.

**Top:** Site manager Scott Simpson watches from a blind at Prairie Ridge State Natural Area in Jasper County.

**Above:** A male greater prairie chicken tries his best to impress a female with his courtship display.

**Right:** After the females have left for the day, male prairie chickens fight over territory.

**Facing page:** Every spring, male prairie chickens try to attract females by inflating bright orange sacs on the sides of their necks. The resulting "boom" sounds like a person blowing across the top of a soda bottle. Prairie chickens probably numbered in the millions when the first settlers arrived in Illinois. Prairie Ridge hosts roughly one-half of Illinois' remaining population of about 200.

A northern harrier hovers over a grassy field between Bath and Patterson Bay, not far from the Illinois River.

An early spring thunderstorm gathers strength over tall grasses at Carpenter Park in Springfield.

# ANDERSON PRAIRIE
## *Restoring Illinois' Past*

I arrived at Pana High School to photograph football practice one August day, just as the coach was sending his players off on a midday break.

With nothing to do for more than an hour, I headed out to the countryside to explore. What I discovered was an Illinois gold mine of native flora and fauna known as Anderson Prairie.

Pulling up the short driveway, I was greeted by Jean and David Nance. Jean teaches at the Illinois School for the Deaf in Jacksonville and David has taught at Pana High School for 23 years. During two recent summers, they have parked their camper at Anderson Prairie and worked to protect and restore this remnant of pre-settlement Illinois.

Prairies are teeming, diverse ecosystems, and Anderson Prairie is no different. It boasts more than 300 plant species, more than 65 bird species and 56 butterfly species. Named for longtime Pana biology teacher Vernon Anderson, it is a 25-acre

tract that was once was a railroad right-of-way. Since the mid-1980s, the Nances and other nature buffs from the area have maintained it as an original Illinois prairie, one of few still existing in the state.

"Returning this piece of land to an orig-inal Illinois prairie has been a dream," says David Nance.

"It's like a living museum, and that's exactly what we're shooting for. There are so few original prairies left."

Keeping natural areas in their natural state requires continued vigilance. "There is immense pressure on natural areas from exotic species of plants that can come in and take over," he says.

A recent federal Environmental Protection Agency cleanup of an old petroleum refining facility bordering the prairie will help. The old storage tanks and their odor are gone, Nance says. A buffer zone of 100 feet or more is planned to further protect the prairie.

A bike trail running through Anderson Prairie will give visitors a closeup look at the prairie. The trail will soon connect to Taylorville and someday Springfield.

"We'll have the longest trail in Illinois in three to four years," Nance says.

**David Nance moves in for a closeup picture of blooming prairie plants at Anderson Prairie.**

**Above: An eastern tiger swallowtail is one of 56 butterfly species counted at the prairie.**

**Left: Thick spike blazing star blooms in Anderson Prairie, home to more than 300 species of native plants.**

**Facing page: A hummingbird clearwing moth gathers nectar from wild bergamot.**

Jean Nance keeps granddaughter Annalise Siegert in tow as she clears woody brush intruding on the prairie.

David and Jean Nance and granddaughter Annalise head back to their camper after a morning of clearing brush at Anderson Prairie.

# NATURE ON THE MOVE
## *The Mysteries of Migration*

Could you make it across the Gulf of Mexico on a single tank of gas?

That ruby-throated hummingbird at your backyard feeder will *have* to get that kind of fantastic mileage. In the fall, hummingbirds fuel up and gain an extra 50 percent of their body weight in preparation for migration. The 18-20 hour trip across the water will use everything they've got.

Migration conjures up mental images of graceful V's of ducks and geese winging their way south. Waterfowl aren't the only ones on the move during this time, however. More than 5 billion birds of all kinds, from sparrows to hawks, cross the United States at the rate of tens of millions each day.

Most people believe that birds migrate because of cold weather, but the real reason is to find a reliable source of food.

Here are some other facts about migrating wildlife:

◆ It is a myth that hummingbirds

**A female ruby-throated hummingbird fuels up at a backyard feeder.**

migrate on the backs of geese. They travel at different times and head to different destinations.

◆ Monarch butterflies are able to find the same forest in Mexico where their great-great grandparents spent the winter. Young monarchs from the United States are able to navigate a route they have never flown to a mountain they have never seen.

◆ Sea turtles return after years in the open ocean to the same sandy beach on which they hatched. Some even have tiny magnetic particles in their bodies that act like compasses.

◆ The arctic tern is considered to have the longest migration route of any bird. It travels 11,000 miles from one pole to the other and back again each year.

◆ All migrating animals, including birds, use a variety of directional cues: Sun and star patterns, smells, landmarks and the Earth's magnetic field. They memorize these signs.

◆ Geographic features, such as mountain ranges, peninsulas and lakes may funnel migrating birds into narrow bands, creating a spectacular display of nature on the move.

Geese fly past the setting sun at Lake Springfield. Following pages: Cedar waxwings flock to feed in hawthorn trees in Rochester's Community Park.

**Above: A monarch butterfly rests on goldenrod at the Jim Edgar Panther Creek State Fish and Wildlife Area.**
**Facing page: Geese gather on the ice at Lake Springfield during spring migration.**

Double-crested cormorants roost in trees along the Lake Springfield shoreline. Their call is a distinctive and eerie *croaak*.

**Participating in the age-old ritual of migration, a Canada goose joins a flock of greater white-fronted geese on New Year's morning 2000.**

# BALD EAGLES: *Symbols of Freedom*

The reaction is always the same:

When people see a bald eagle, they almost always react with sheer delight.

Perhaps folks are aware of how lucky we are that our national symbol has been able to recover from the brink of extinction. Maybe the eagle's majestic size and brilliant white head attract us. Whatever the reason, to make a group of wildlife watchers happy, just show them an adult bald eagle.

Eagles have become so popular that festivals and special events have sprung up around their winter visits to Illinois waterways. Event organizers always fret that warm weather will disperse the eagles up and down the riverbank. They fear the eagles won't be forced to congregate near locks and dams where water remains open and people will be gathered.

Organizers apologize if the trees are not filled with eagles: "You should have been

**Eagle watchers spot a bald eagle in the Mark Twain National Wildlife Refuge near Grafton.**

here last week," they say. But apologies are completely unnecessary. Scanning the crowd, one can see children and grandparents alike smiling and pointing as they spot a lone bald eagle fishing below the dam.

At the Illinois Waterway Visitors Center at the Starved Rock Lock and Dam on the Illinois River, powerful spotting scopes pro-

vided for Eagle Watching Weekend gave people astonishing closeup views. The birds appeared to be so close that it was possible to meet an eagle's gaze head-on from more than 100 yards away.

It is gratifying that interest in the winter visits of bald eagles remains high even as the birds are poised to be removed from the federal endangered species list.

Judging from the convoys of vehicles on eagle tours and hundreds of visitors at weekend festivals, interest in our native wildlife — and especially eagles — is continuing to grow.

Conservationists will tell you that it is difficult to persuade people to protect things they have never seen. Getting people to venture outside to see our national symbol is the first step in the effort to reintroduce our citizens to the variety and beauty of Illinois wildlife.

Head for an Illinois waterway this winter with your family. Teach your children about the wonders of nature. And when you spot a bald eagle together, be sure to share your child's delight.

An immature bald eagle (upper right) and a pair of adults perch in a tree overlooking the Starved Rock Lock and Dam on the Illinois River. In cold weather, eagles congregate near dams where open water remains for fishing.

A bald eagle surveys its surroundings near the Illinois River bridge in downtown Meredosia.

**Three immature bald eagles soar past the rising moon near Naples.**

**Above: The face-painting booth is popular with kids during Eagle Watching Weekend. The Illinois Waterway Visitors Center at Starved Rock Lock and Dam hosts the event in January.**

**Left: A bald eagle takes to the skies near Meredosia. Bald eagles have become important tourist draws for river communities. Many towns have started festivals celebrating their unique winter visitors.**

Before a panel of its peers, an immature bald eagle makes a perfect landing on a dead tree branch near Naples. Once near extinction, bald eagles will soon be removed from the federal endangered species list.

**A double-crested cormorant comes up with a fish dinner during a migration stopover near Lincoln Memorial Garden.**

**Canada goose goslings dutifully follow their parents on a twilight cruise across Lake Springfield.**

**Turtles near the Lake Springfield Wildlife Sanctuary discover that an exposed tree trunk is a fine place to bask in the sun.**

**Mallard ducks settle in for the night along Lake Springfield's shoreline.**

A great blue heron, its legs trailing behind, soars through a sunset sky above Sangchris Lake State Park.

An American coot scoops up a morsel of food from the mirrorlike surface of Lake Springfield.

# WILD IN THE CITY

**A house wren leaves home in search of insects.**

How well do you know your neighbors? I mean really *know* your neighbors? I'm not talking about the nice man next door who is always working in his garden. I mean the residents that live *in* the garden — or maybe *above* the garden in that giant oak tree.

Those house wrens in the birdhouse next door might be better neighbors than you think. They provide, at no charge, beautiful songs to counteract the lawn mowers, weed whackers and other white noise of civilization. They also spend the entire day catching insects for their hungry brood.

What pals!

Goldfinches, indigo buntings and cardinals add a splash of color to the yard. So do the butterflies that flutter above our gardens.

In recent years, bird-watching, bird feeding and other nature-related activities have grown into some of our most popular pastimes.

As civilization expands, more and more wildlife seems to adapt to urban life as well. Barred owls, Cooper's hawks, raccoons, opossums and white-tailed deer are among the species that have found homes in urban and suburban areas.

Maybe they have been here all along. It could be we're just beginning to take notice of the variety of life in our own back yards.

We're learning it's worth the time to really get to know our neighbors.

An acrobatic squirrel hangs upside down to reach ears of corn on a squirrel feeder. Depending on whom you ask, squirrels are either a bane or a delight to backyard bird feeders.

On a cold winter morning, a blue jay dines at a backyard bird feeder. Birdwatching and other nature-related activities are among the most popular pastimes in the United States.

A white-breasted nuthatch comes down the trunk of a tree head-first. Nuthatches are common birds found in woodlands as well as back yards.

A female downy woodpecker (left) gives a peanut to her seemingly larger chick.

A mother raccoon and her brood emerge from a storm drain at dusk near Lincoln Park. Raccoons are among the wildlife species that have adapted well to civilization.

# THE LOST BRIDGE TRAIL

Give Mother Nature an inch, and she might just take 5 miles.

Stop, look and listen along the Lost Bridge Trail, the 5-mile recreational path created on an unused railroad line between Springfield and Rochester.

Turn around just in time, and you'll catch a glimpse of an eastern chipmunk — bushy tail held high — as it disappears into the grass.

Look toward the highway and watch goldfinches snack on thistle seed as commuters rush home to Rochester.

**The Lost Bridge Trail parallels busy Illinois 29 for much of its 5-mile route.**

And, if you're really quiet, peer through the trees and try to sneak a peek at a great blue heron or great egret fishing in a pond.

The Lost Bridge Trail is tucked so close to well-traveled Illinois 29 that hikers often see and hear the traffic. Despite the close proximity to one of civilization's busy corridors, a variety of living things call the area home.

Opened late in 1997, the trail now carries bicyclists, inline skaters, hikers and walkers from the Illinois Department of Transportation complex on Dirksen Parkway to Rochester Station.

Take your time when you're on the trail. Look closely and you might see some of your wild neighbors who make their home here.

**A goldfinch snacks on thistle seed along Illinois Route 29 between Rochester and Springfield.**

**An eastern chipmunk ventures onto the Lost Bridge Trail during the last remaining minutes of daylight.**

**Top:** No, it's not a monarch. Viceroy butterflies mimic the look of monarchs in hopes that birds and other predators will think they taste just as bad.

**Above:** The familiar "Chick-a-dee-dee-dee" call gives away this little guy in the black cap.

**Left:** Inline skaters cruise the trail.

**A spider waits patiently in its web along the edge of the Lost Bridge Trail.**

The setting sun highlights foxtail grasses growing next to the trail.

A northern cardinal tries to stay out of sight at the trail's edge.

**Above:** All appears quiet in winter. Closer inspection, though, reveals a downy woodpecker searching for insect eggs and other treats in the bark of a tree.

**Right:** A pair of bicycle tire tracks are the only signs of activity after a winter snowfall.

On safari in Olney City Park, I came armed with enough camera gear to make a National Geographic photographer jealous. I sat stealthily on a picnic table — telephoto lens in hand — quietly hoping for a glimpse of the famous Olney white squirrel.

Finally I saw one, but it was too far away to photograph. Suddenly, one particularly brave white squirrel appeared and headed my way. He kept coming closer and closer, then jumped up on the table and plunked himself down right next to me (facing page).

Needless to say, I felt pretty stupid with all that fancy equipment.

It turns out that I was sitting just out of sight of the park's feeding station, where squirrels congregate to gorge themselves on corn and birdseed scattered for their benefit by the townspeople.

Olney's albino squirrels are gray squirrels with defective genes.

"In every mammal, genetics sometimes go awry and one is born albino or white," says John Stencel, retired biology professor

**The intersection of White Squirrel Drive and White Squirrel Circle is in Olney City Park.**

at Olney Central College. "It happens in deer, in birds; it happens even in people."

Since 1902, the unusual rodents have been a fixture in this small town (pop. 9,000 people and just over 100 white squirrels.)

White squirrel banners line the business district and their likeness is emblazoned on police cars.

While it would be difficult for a white squirrel to hide from predators in the wild, Olney forms a somewhat protective environment. City residents are encouraged to take extra care when driving on city streets,

and scouts have erected nest boxes and feeding stations.

The white squirrel population appears to be holding steady. Stencel organized a yearly count, held on three consecutive Saturdays in October, for more than 20 years.

About 40 volunteers divide the town into sections and head out at daybreak to count squirrels. In 1999, an average of 115 white squirrels was recorded.

Stencel, who taught for 40 years, retired at the end of the 1999-2000 school year. He has trained colleagues to take over the monitoring of the white squirrel population. Reflecting on his years as head of white squirrel headquarters, Stencel says the count has been a lot of work — but "maybe I've made a little contribution."

Since I didn't offer any contributions to the white squirrel on that picnic table, he quickly turned out to be a fair weather friend. In a moment he was off again, this time in search of a tourist carrying something more valuable than cameras. French fries would do.

A white squirrel in
Olney City Park
poses for a portrait.
Olney's unusual
population of white
squirrels is its
claim to fame.

**Above:** A white squirrel savors its prize, a french fry handed out by a visitor to Olney City Park.

**Left:** A white squirrel provides the perfect photo opportunity for Bernice Mayfield of Largo, Fla., who was in Olney visiting family.

**Facing page:** White squirrel banners line this Olney city street.

Above: This white squirrel was seen romping at Olney City Park. Data collected by students and other volunteers showed the white squirrel population has been holding steady.

Facing page: Gray and white squirrels sit side by side. The white squirrels are albino — gray squirrels with defective genes.

Right: Professor John Stencel organized the annual white squirrel count for more than 20 years. He has now retired after 40 years of teaching, 34 at Olney Central College.

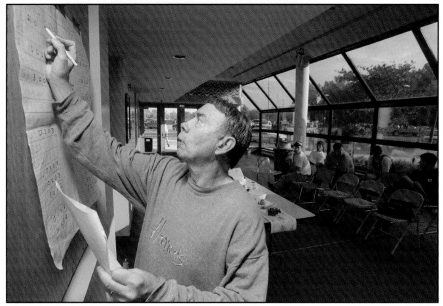

# A PHOTOGRAPHER'S JOURNAL

## A Pictorial History of the Illinois Raptor Center

Everyone has heard the story of the ugly duckling, right? Well, *this* fairy tale is even more compelling, because it involves a homely little owl chick — orphaned when its tree was cut down — and how it eventually blossomed into a beautiful barn owl, an Illinois endangered species.

With barn owls all but gone from Illinois, volunteers at the Illinois Raptor Center were excited to be able to help a species in peril. Of the two chicks discovered in the felled tree, one survived to adulthood and a second chance at life.

Since 1994, I have had the opportunity to document many such stories in my role as volunteer photographer for the wildlife education and rehabilitation center in Decatur.

Formerly known as Wildlife CPR, the organization has grown to encompass a 15-acre wildlife center, admit between 700-950 animals each year to its wildlife hospital and deliver educational programs all over Illinois.

Birds of prey that are used for education are permanently disabled in some way, meaning they cannot hunt, fly or survive on their own. These birds receive frequent handling and training to prepare them for their new role as educators.

They also provide fascinating subjects for photography, because it would be nearly impossible — and often dangerous — to be close enough to take these kinds of pictures in the wild.

**Illinois Raptor Center director Jane Seitz evaluates the barn owl chicks.**

**This Illinois state-endangered barn owl chick was left homeless after the tree housing its nest was cut down.**

Top: The gangly chick grew into a beautiful adult barn owl. Above and right: The owl was released on the same farm near Harvel where it was found. The Illinois Raptor Center's Jacques Nuzzo carried the bird up a ladder and placed it in a nest box mounted inside the barn.

# FACES IN THE CROWD

These birds have, at one time or another, passed through the doors of the Illinois Raptor Center. Severe injuries kept them from being released. Clockwise from top left: bald eagle, saw whet owl, great horned owl, barred owl and Cooper's hawk.

**Many of these birds are the stars of the Illinois Raptor Center's educational programs. Clockwise from top left: American kestrel, peregrine falcon, long-eared owl, juvenile red-tailed hawk and golden eagle.**

Below: Fairgoers react when Shawnee, a short-eared owl, delivers her characteristic "bark" during a program at the 1998 Illinois State Fair (left). Illinois Raptor Center volunteers present educational programs all over Illinois. Birds of prey used for education have been permanently injured and are not able to live on their own.

Thousands of volunteer hours go into caring for animals, like these baby cottontail rabbits, admitted to the wildlife hospital portion of the Illinois Raptor Center. Top row: A red-tailed hawk's wing is examined; volunteer Dean Ater installs a squirrel nest box; cleanup is a daily chore.

A pair of common loons are released at Lake Shelbyville by Illinois Raptor Center volunteers. To water birds in flight, large expanses of concrete can look like bodies of water; these loons made that mistake and landed in the middle of a highway. These heavy, forward-leaning birds require water for taking off. Center volunteers observed the loons for a couple of days to be sure they were uninjured, then released them into the lake.

**Jacques Nuzzo releases a rehabilitated barred owl at Rhodes France Scout Reservation near Pana.**

# TECHNICAL INFORMATION

On this particular day, a pair of white-tailed deer didn't feel like posing for pictures. As soon as my car came around the corner, they took off — waving goodbye to me with their big white tails.

That's a pretty accurate snapshot of an average day in the life of a nature photographer. It's also what makes this kind of photography fun and challenging. When your subjects do cooperate, it can be most rewarding.

Judging from the many questions I receive at the newspaper, nature watchers and photographers in central Illinois want to know what goes into making good photographs.

Camera equipment includes Canon EOS-1 cameras, and most often, a 500mm *f*4.5 lens with a 1.4x teleconverter. That gives an effective focal length of 700mm and a wide-open aperture of *f*6.3. Film is mostly Fujicolor 200.

A variety of other lenses are sometimes used, from a 20mm wide-angle to long telephotos. A Nikon 8008 camera and Nikon lenses are in the camera bag I carry

**What nature photographers usually see.**

in my off hours.

In a few instances, I've used a remote trigger. This approach allows the camera to be present while I sit inside, sip a cup of coffee and wait for birds and squirrels to

come to my feeders. (I highly recommend this technique in winter!)

The only pictures in this book taken from a blind are of the prairie chickens in Jasper County. Most of the time, my car provides a suitable blind. Wild birds and animals seem to tolerate cars passing by on the road; as long as I stay in or near my car, I'm free to photograph.

If the animal is going about its business, unconcerned about my presence, I feel I've found a comfortable distance. That's not to say I wouldn't like to be closer, but through experience I've learned that a "comfort zone" exists.

When photographing a nest, I avoid going back more than one or two times. I stay on trails and I don't trespass. Pass up the potential picture if you must blaze a new trail to a nest site. Any trail you need to create for yourself can also clear the way for predators to easily reach the babies.

Lastly, don't underestimate the value of finding a comfortable spot and sitting quietly.

After awhile, you may be rewarded.

The white squirrels in Olney City Park wouldn't come near my camera rigged at the park's feeding station. The other squirrels didn't give it a second thought.

# ACKNOWLEDGMENTS

*A special word of thanks to the following for their contributions:*

SUE and ED MAHONEY,
RON and MARY BETH VOSE
for the many photo tips and for the
use of your back yards

◆

JANE SEITZ,
JACQUES NUZZO
and BETH FLITZ
of the Illinois Raptor Center,
Decatur

◆

H. DAVID BOHLEN,
assistant curator,
The Illinois State Museum

◆

DAVE ROBSON,
horticulturist,
Sangamon Extension Service

◆

ERIC GRIMM,
curator of botany,
The Illinois State Museum

◆

SCOTT SIMPSON,
natural heritage biologist
and site manager,
Prairie Ridge State Natural Area

DAVID and JEAN NANCE,
Anderson Prairie

◆

JOHN STENCEL,
professor of biology, retired,
Olney Central College

◆

PATRICK COBURN,
publisher,

BARRY J. LOCHER,
editor,
and the employees of
The State Journal-Register

◆

Editing assistance provided by
DAVE BAKKE, TED WOLF,
LINDA FRAEMBS and
ROSALYNNE HARTY;
supplemental reporting
by RALPH LOOS

◆

Design by
KATHLEEN RILEY

*Thanks to the many readers who phoned and
e-mailed tips for photos. Many of the pictures
generated by your calls are in this book.*

**Sue and Ed Mahoney's back yard is landscaped exclusively for bird habitat.**

**Facing page: Black-eyed Susans provide plenty of summer color at the Lincoln Memorial Garden Ostermeier Prairie.**

# ABOUT THE PHOTOGRAPHER

Rich Saal

Chris Young has been a photojournalist for The State Journal-Register in Springfield, Ill., since 1990. An Iowa native, he holds a B.A. in journalism from Iowa State University. He has worked for The Des Moines Register and was with the Omaha World Herald for five years before coming to Springfield.

Young has received a variety of awards for photography from the National Press Photographers Association, The Associated Press, Illinois Press Association and Illinois Press Photographers Association.

He is a former Illinois and Nebraska Photographer of the Year and twice was runner-up for that award in the Iowa, Illinois, Wisconsin and Minnesota region of the National Press Photographers Association.

Young is a four-time winner of the James S. Copley Ring of Truth Award, given to journalists working for all Copley Press newspapers.

In 1997, Young's photograph of comet Hale-Bopp soaring over the carillon in Washington Park was produced by The State Journal-Register as a poster. It sold in excess of 25,000 copies.

Young lives in Springfield with his wife Kathleen and 2-year-old daughter Clara, who is already accustomed to having her picture taken. Unlike her father's wildlife subjects, Clara often says, "More pictures, please!"